100

Great
KITCHENS &
BATHROOMS

by Architects

100

Great
KITCHENS &
BATHROOMS
by Architects

images
Publishing

Published in Australia in 2008 by
The Images Publishing Group Pty Ltd
ABN 89 059 734 431
6 Bastow Place, Mulgrave, Victoria, 3170, Australia
Tel: +61 3 9561 5544 Fax: +61 3 9561 4860
books@imagespublishing.com
www.imagespublishing.com

Copyright © The Images Publishing Group Pty Ltd 2008
The Images Publishing Group Reference Number: 780

Cataloguing-in-Publication data for this title is available from the National Library of Australia

ISBN: 978 1 86470 307 8

Edited by Andrew Hall

Designed by The Graphic Image Studio Pty Ltd, Mulgrave, Australia
www.tgis.com.au

Pre-publishing services by Splitting Image Colour Studio, Pty Ltd, Australia

Printed by Everbest Printing Co. Ltd., in Hong Kong/China

IMAGES has included on its website a page for special notices in relation to this and our other
publications. Please visit www.imagespublishing.com.

KITCHENS

"The double-height space brings light into the kitchen from all directions" MCINTURFF ARCHITECTS

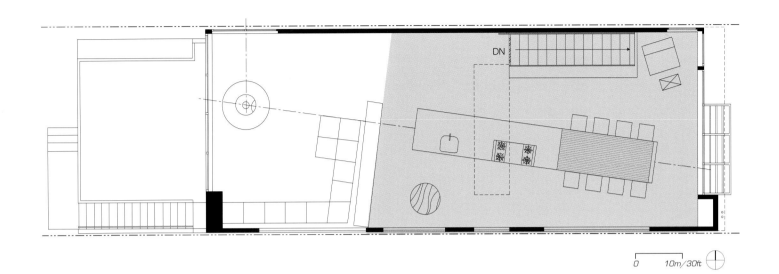

0   10m/30ft

"Stainless steel assemblage extends to become the walnut dining table" CCS ARCHITECTURE

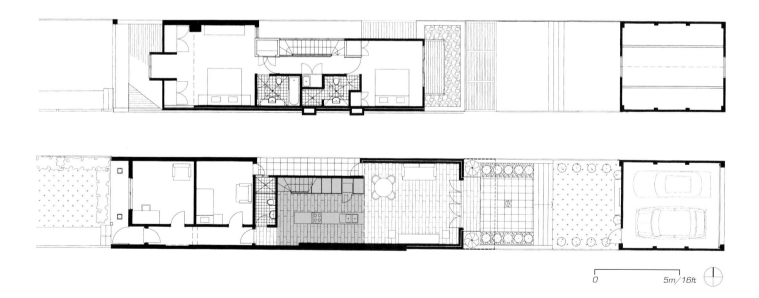

0   5m/16ft

11

"Servery and suspended range hood form sculptural elements" CULLEN FENG

12

"Large sliding panel screens kitchen from living and dining area" STANIC HARDING

0   3m/10ft

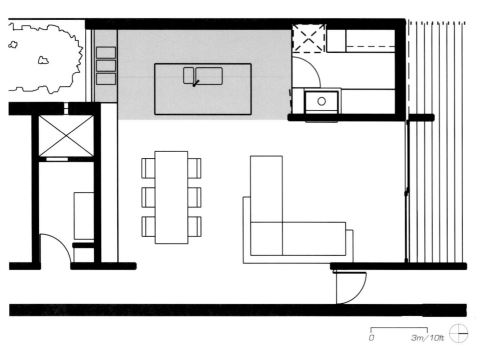

0   3m/10ft

"Work bench is large" STEPHEN JOLSON ARCHITECT PTY LTD

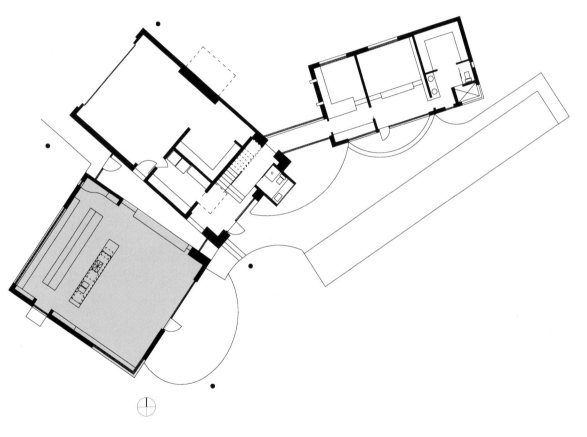

"A native mesquite wood counter complements the birch cabinets" IBARRA ROSANO DESIGN ARCHITECTS

"Continuous use of stainless steel on curved wall, fixtures, and appliances" GRAFT

"Wooden sliding wall opens the kitchen to the living areas" OFIS ARHITEKTI

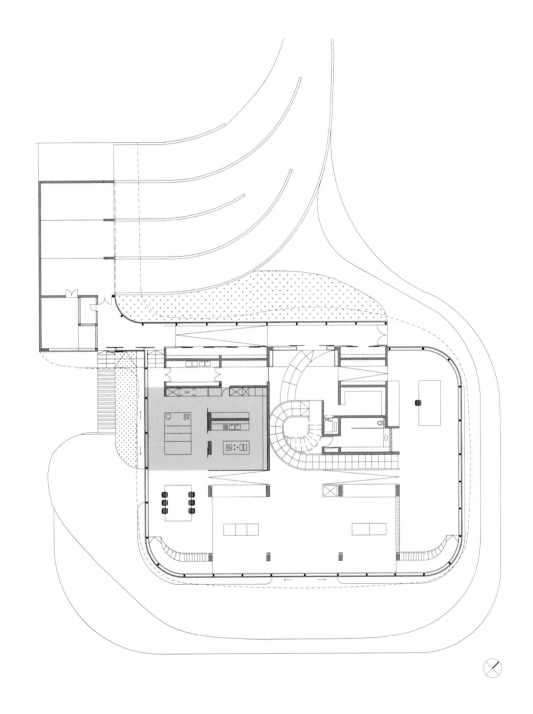

26

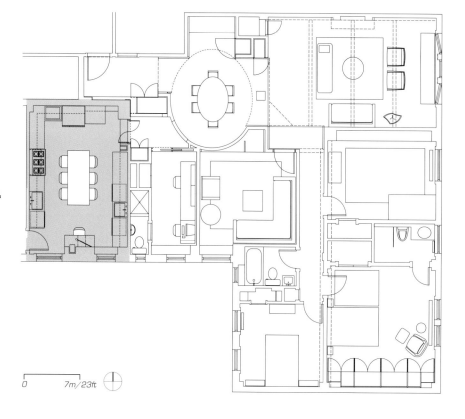

0   7m/23ft

"Cabinets line the perimeter, maximizing the kitchen space" RESOLUTION:4 ARCHITECTURE

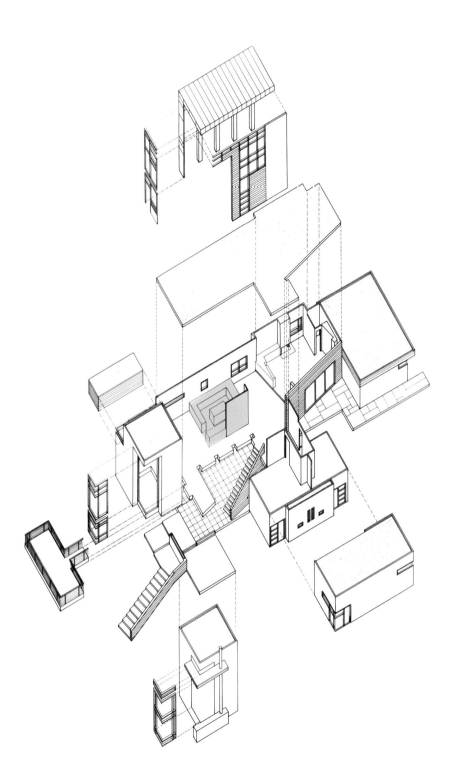

"There are views in every direction" STUDIO 9ONE2 ARCHITECTURE

"Opening to patio establishes connections to landscape" CCS ARCHITECTURE

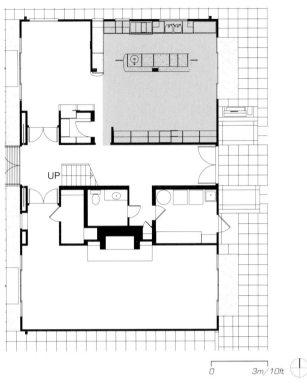

UP

0   3m/10ft

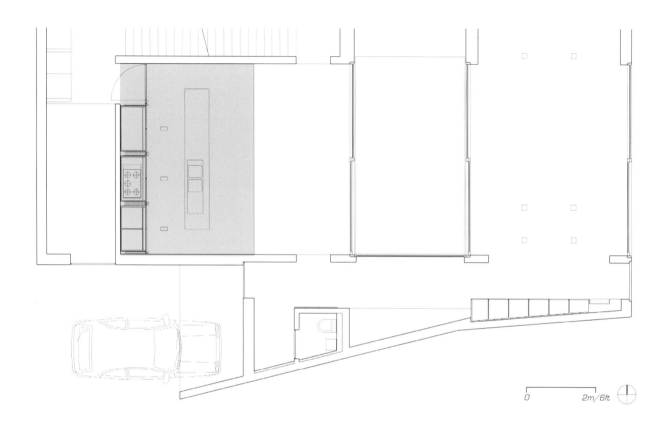

0   2m/6ft

"Shelving and cooking are concealed behind sliding doors" ARCHITECTENLAB

"Style is casual and cottage-like" GOOD ARCHITECTURE

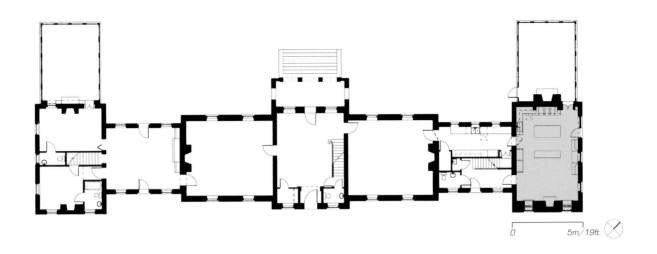

37

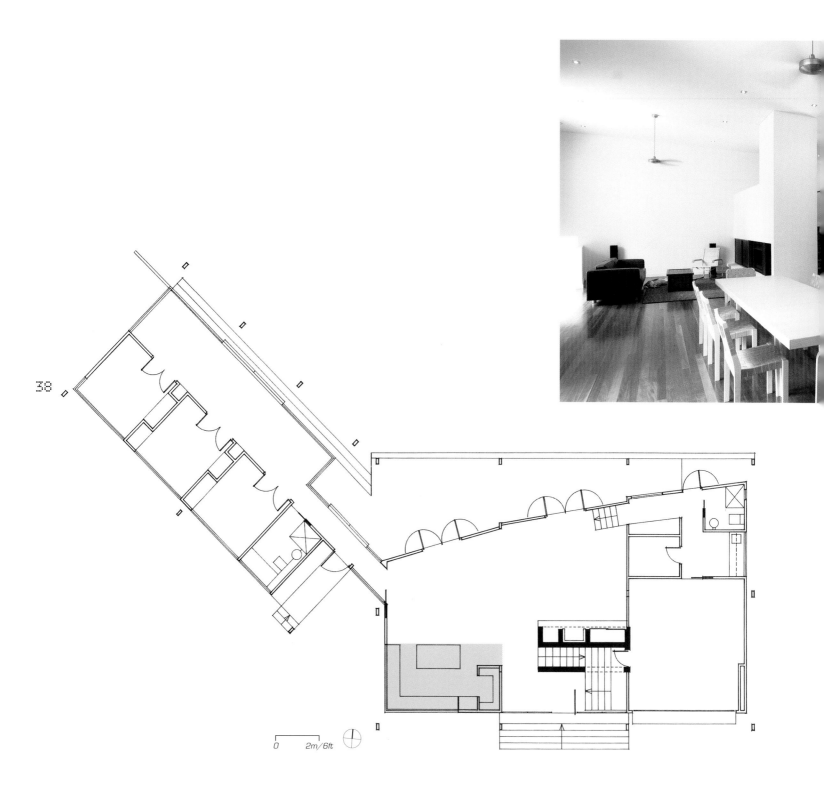

0   2m/6ft

"Counter and overhead cupboards frame the view to the garden" CONNOR + SOLOMON ARCHITECTS

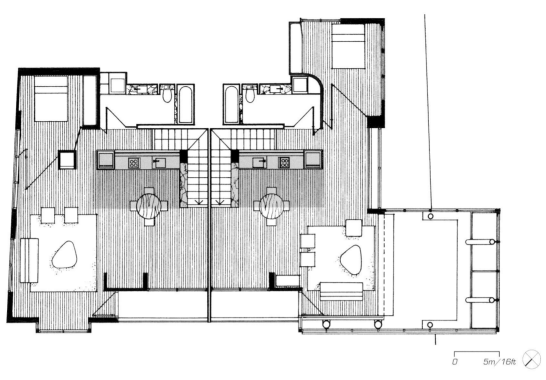

0   5m/16ft

"Translucent splashback brings light to stairwell behind" STANIC HARDING

"Island and dining table appear stage-like against the backdrop of cabinets" RESOLUTION:4 ARCHITECTURE

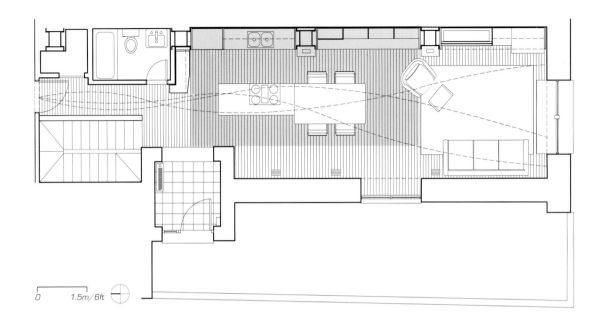

0 1.5m/6ft

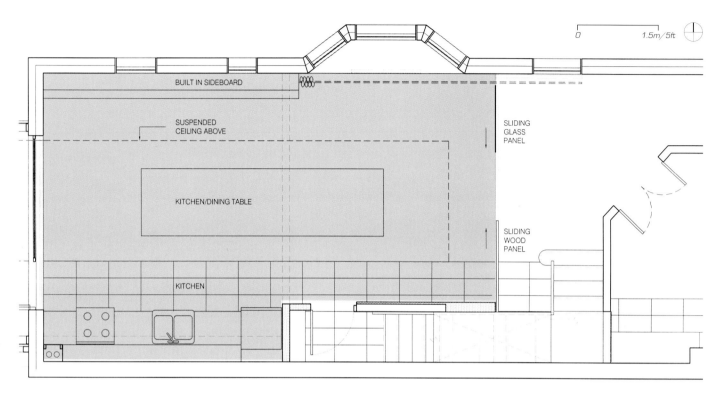

BUILT IN SIDEBOARD

SUSPENDED
CEILING ABOVE

SLIDING
GLASS
PANEL

KITCHEN/DINING TABLE

SLIDING
WOOD
PANEL

KITCHEN

0   1.5m/5ft

"Caters for everyday family living as well as great entertaining" 3RD UNCLE DESIGN

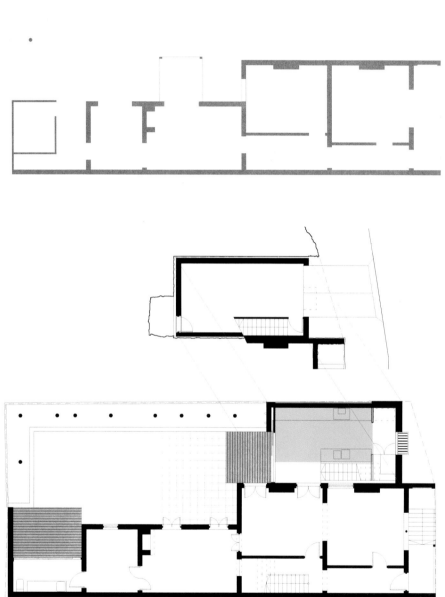

0   1.5m/5ft

"Massive concrete bench structures shape the interior language" CONNOR + SOLOMON ARCHITECTS

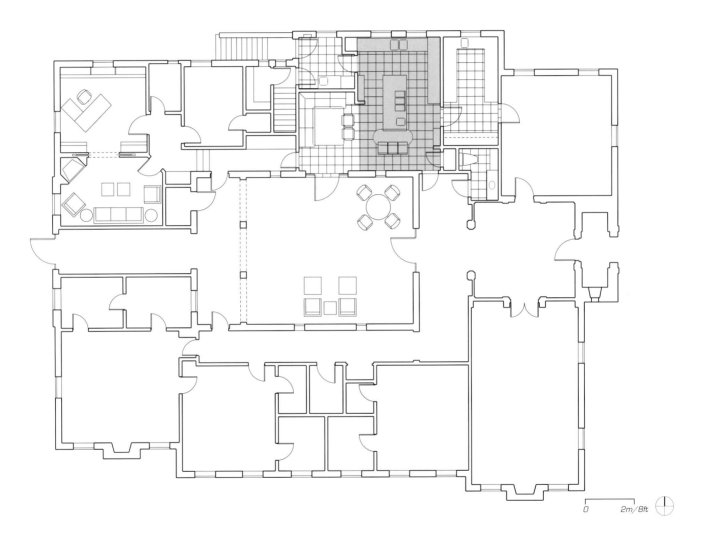

49

"Custom-made island is the heart of the kitchen" RONALD FRINK ARCHITECTS

0 2m/6ft

"The kitchen is not defined by walls" STEPHEN JOLSON ARCHITECT PTY LTD

"Kitchen table adds flexibility to the space" SUPERKÜL INC ARCHITECT

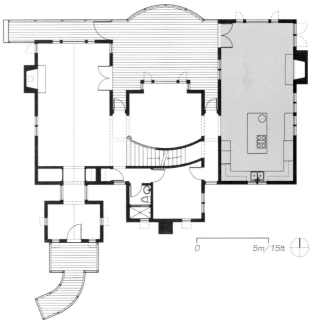

"There are views of the garden through the main window" GOOD ARCHITECTURE

0   5m/15ft

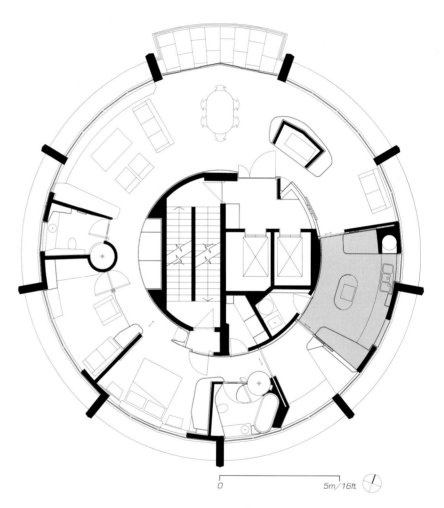

0   5m/16ft

"Central curved island unit contains storage below and range hood above" STANIC HARDING

62

"180-year-old spotted-gum timber benches look like stacked blocks" STEPHEN JOLSON ARCHITECT PTY LTD

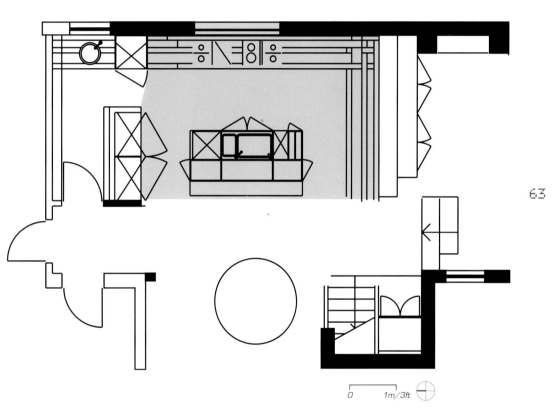

0   1m/3ft

64

"Off-the-shelf materials like plywood and plastic laminate have been used creatively" ARCHIMANIA

"*The good-sized kitchen island is great for parties*" SUPERKÜL INC ARCHITECT

"Volumetric play between cherry cabinetry and stainless steel appliances" CHA & INNERHOFER ARCHITECTURE + DESIGN

"Mirrors lining the walls visually enlarge the compact space" DAVID HICKS PTY LTD

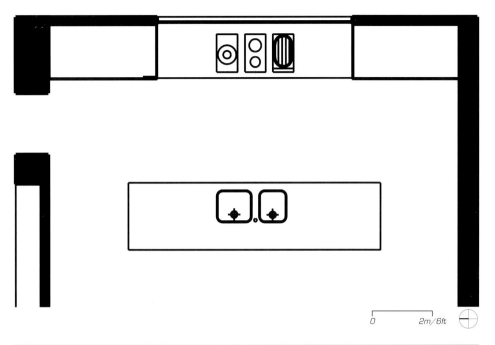

"Glass splashback offers view into uplit bamboo garden" STEPHEN JOLSON ARCHITECT PTY LTD

"Jarrah, veneer, and granite contrast warmly with black glass tiles" IREDALE PEDERSEN HOOK ARCHITECTS

0   6m/20ft

"The bench continues the lines of the architecture" PARSONSON ARCHITECTS

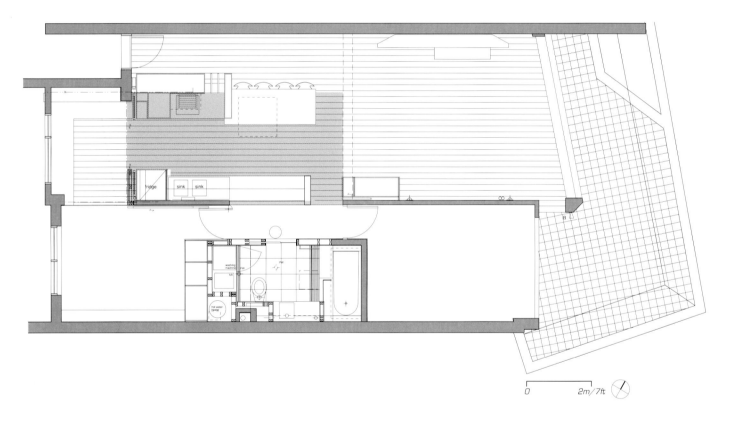

0   2m/7ft

"Kitchen frames view" STANIC HARDING

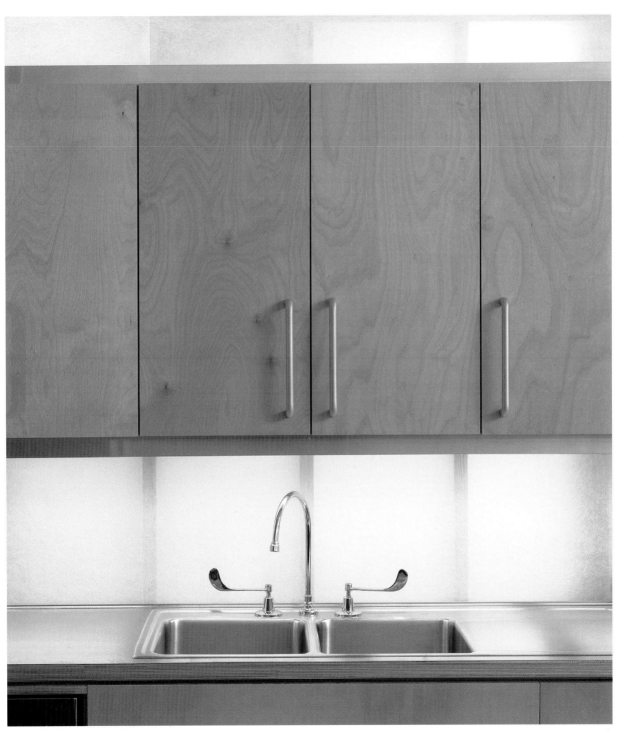

"Simple materials have been arranged to create a modern custom kitchen" RESOLUTION:4 ARCHITECTURE

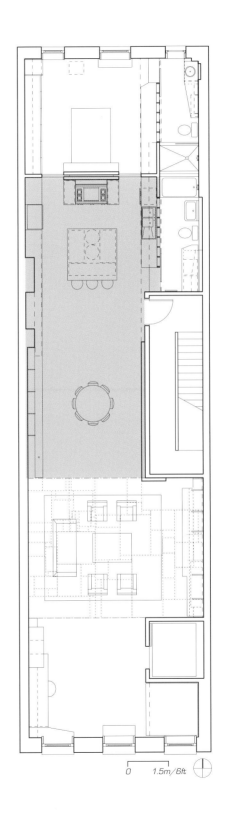

0   1.5m/6ft

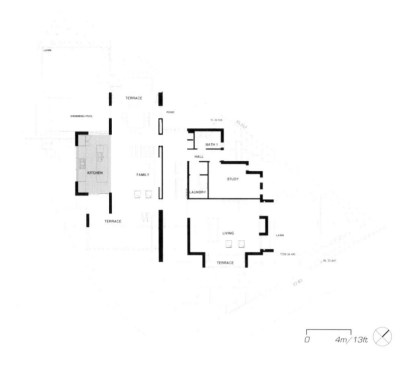

KITCHEN

FAMILY

TERRACE

TERRACE

SWIMMING POOL

LAWN

POND

RL 34.500

BATH 1

HALL

STUDY

LAUNDRY

LIVING

LAWN

TERRACE

TOW 34.440

RL 33.800

0   4m/13ft

"Kitchen enjoys views to harbor" CORBEN

"Joinery forms a picture-frame around cooking activity zone" INTERLANDI MANTESSO ARCHITECTS

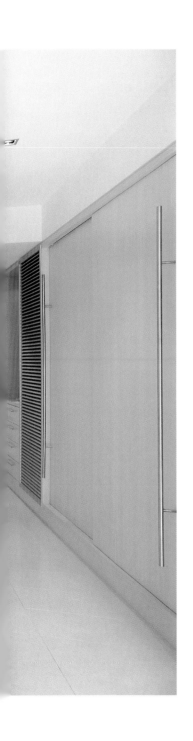

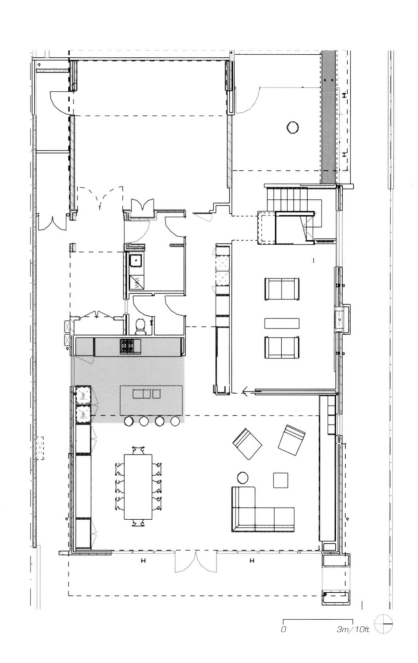

0   3m/10ft

0   2m/6ft

"The kitchen is a sculptural element within the apartment" STANIC HARDING

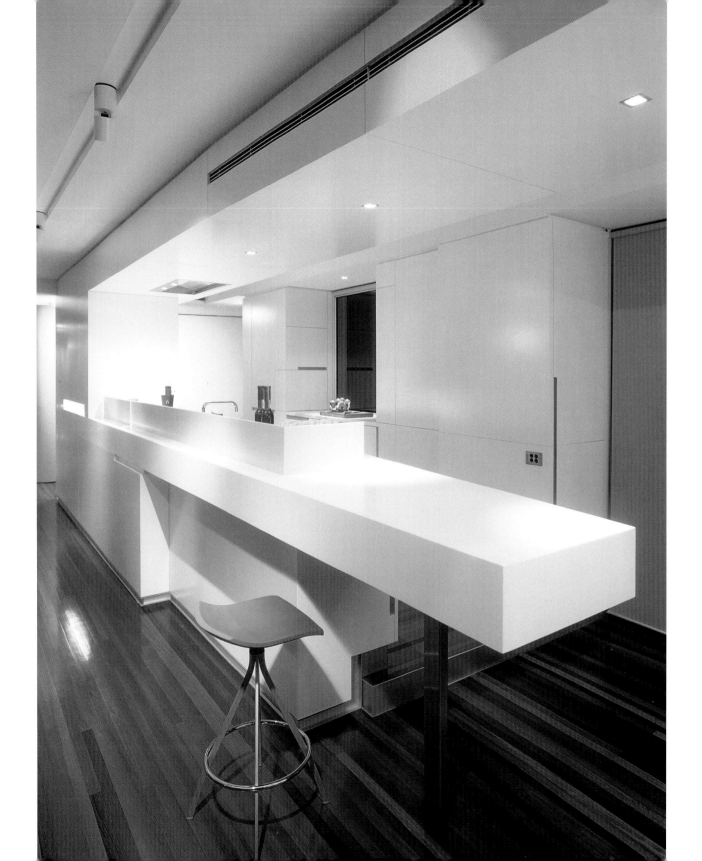

"Central kitchen is accessible to outdoors and owners' art collection"
SHUBIN + DONALDSON ARCHITECTS

"Island bench is multifunctional and storage is concealed" POD INTERIOR DESIGN

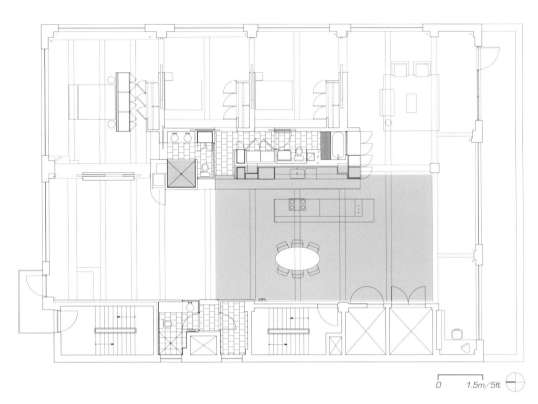

0   1.5m/5ft

"Teak island doubles as a piece of furniture" RESOLUTION:4 ARCHITECTURE

"The earthy tones meld modern and Mexican elements" SHUBIN + DONALDSON ARCHITECTS

"The space is neat and compact" RESOLUTION:4 ARCHITECTURE

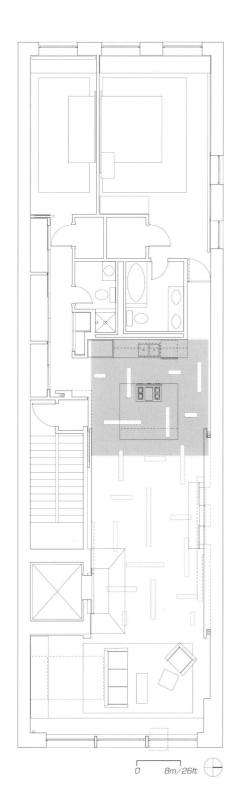

105

"The ceiling has a downward flow" DALE JONES-EVANS PTY LTD ARCHITECTURE

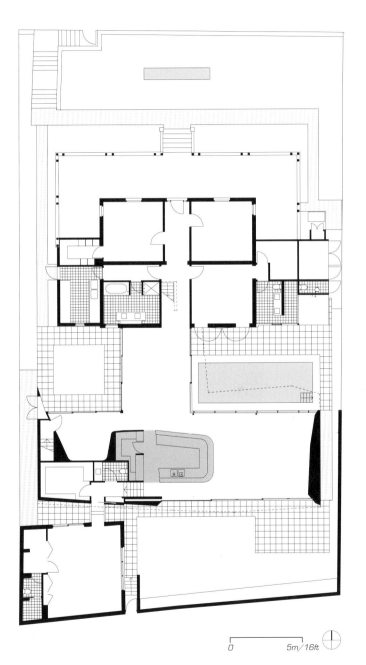

0   5m/16ft

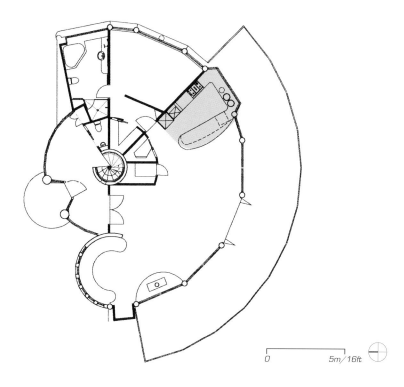

"Embracing sensational views" MURRAY COCKBURN PARTNERSHIP

"Use of white complements natural timbers and stone" BRENT HULENA

"1950's diner area adds enhancement" MARK CUTLER DESIGN

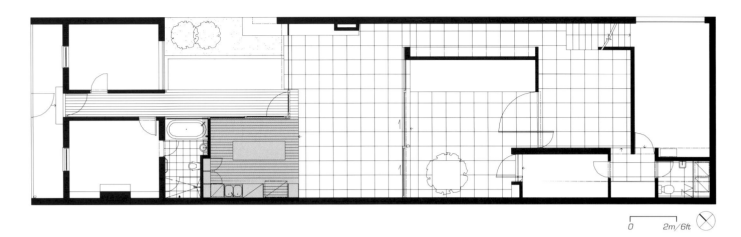

"External walls slide away extending the kitchen into the courtyard" COY & YIONTIS

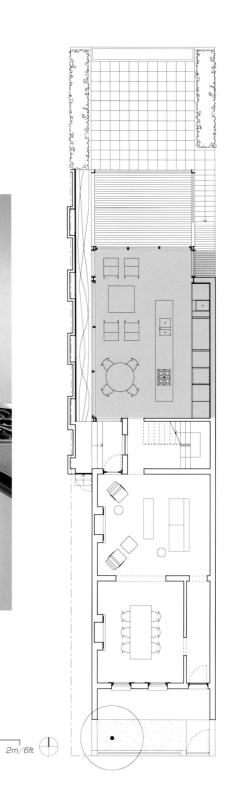

0   2m/6ft

"Kitchen extends beyond the glass line into an outdoor room" ENGELEN MOORE

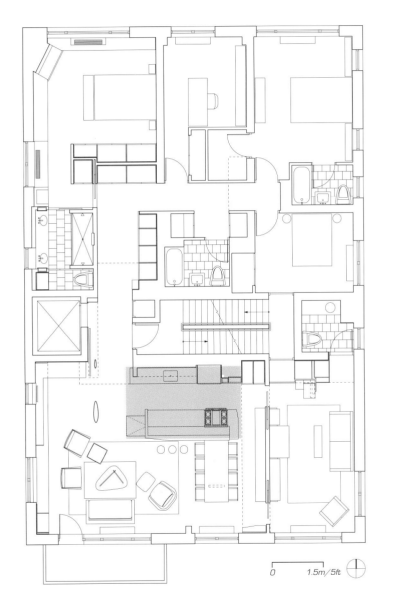

"Integrated dining table and kitchen island demarcate zones of use" RESOLUTION:4 ARCHITECTURE

"Generous space allows for informal entertaining while cooking" CCS ARCHITECTURE

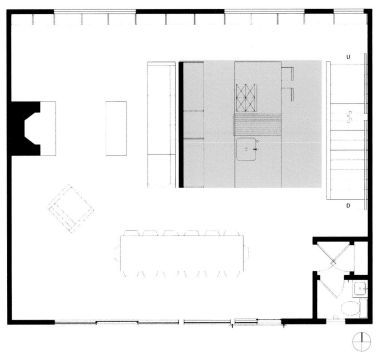

"Functional furniture located within the concrete elements of stair and upstands" INDYK ARCHITECTS

BATHROOMS

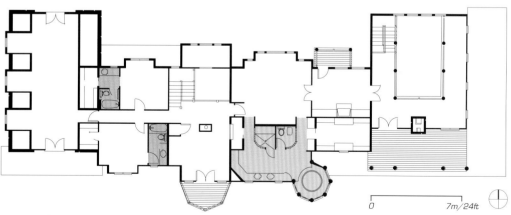

"The use of windows adds natural light to an otherwise dark space" DUBBE-MOULDER ARCHITECTS, PC

"Silver wall cladding is detailed to visually enlarge the small space" DAVID HICKS PTY LTD

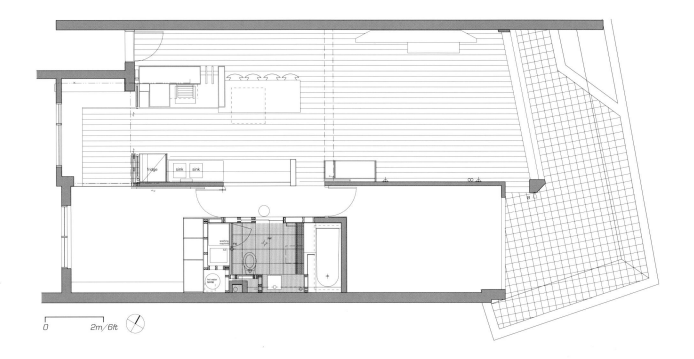

fridge   sink   sink

washing machine

hot water heater

0   2m/6ft

"Only two materials have been used: Corian and limestone" STANIC HARDING

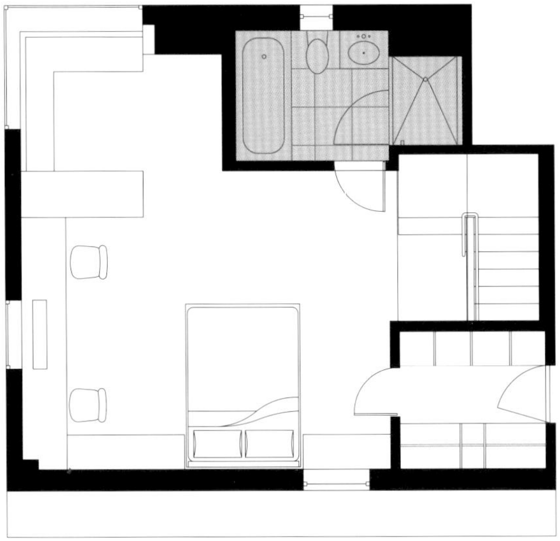

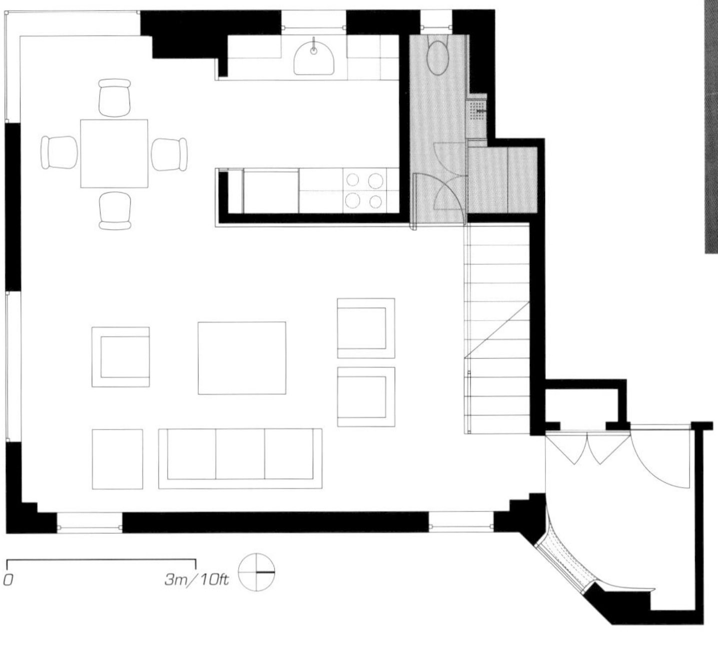

132

0   3m/10ft

"Clean lines result in a soothing atmosphere" CHO SLADE ARCHITECTURE

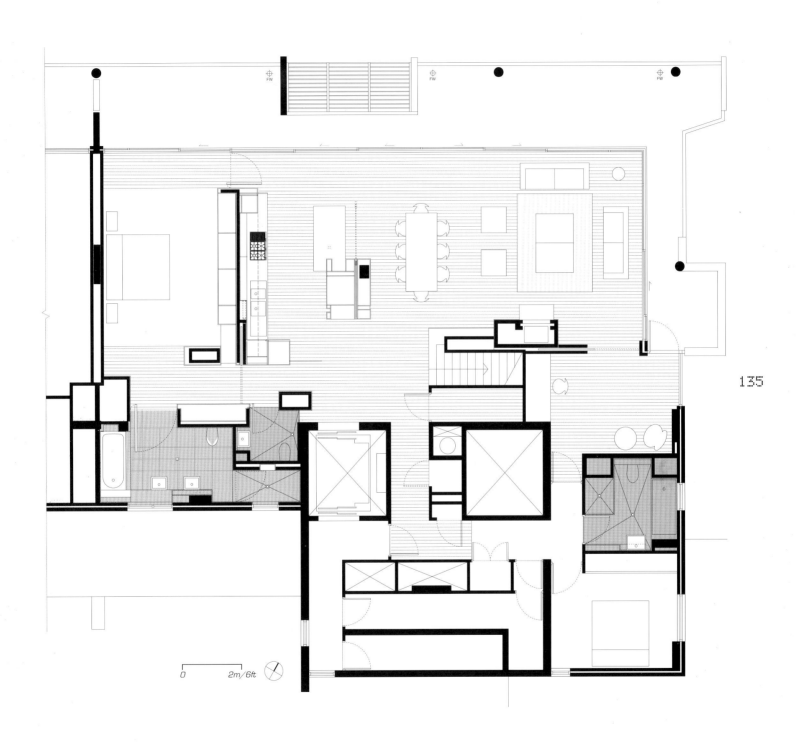

135

"Mirror extends space and appears to double the length of the window" STANIC HARDING

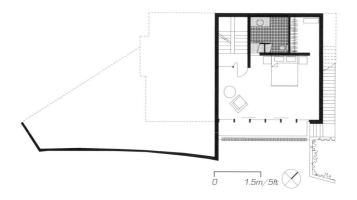

0   1.5m/5ft

"Combination of rough board form concrete, French limestone, and mosaic" STUDIO 0.10 ARCHITECTS

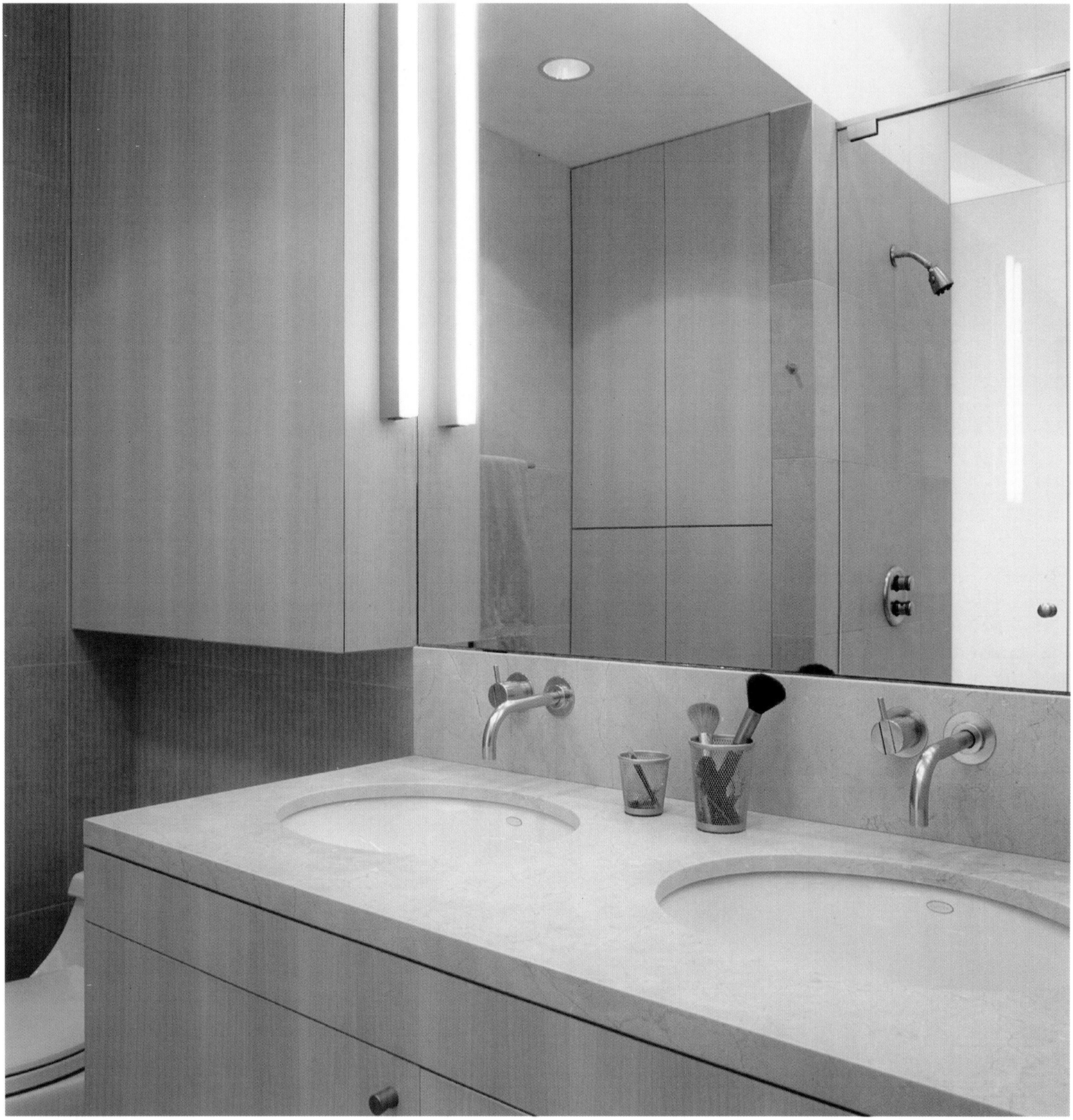

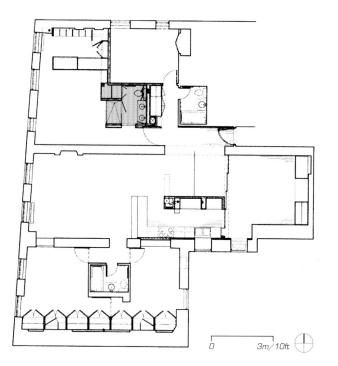

139

"Natural light is maximized" CHO SLADE ARCHITECTURE

"Mirrors extend space and reflect light into hallway via circular shower screen" STANIC HARDING

"Light reflects off glass, mirrors, and water" BOCHSLER & PARTNERS

"Bathroom becomes an extended living room with the use of glass for walls" OFIS ARHITEKTI

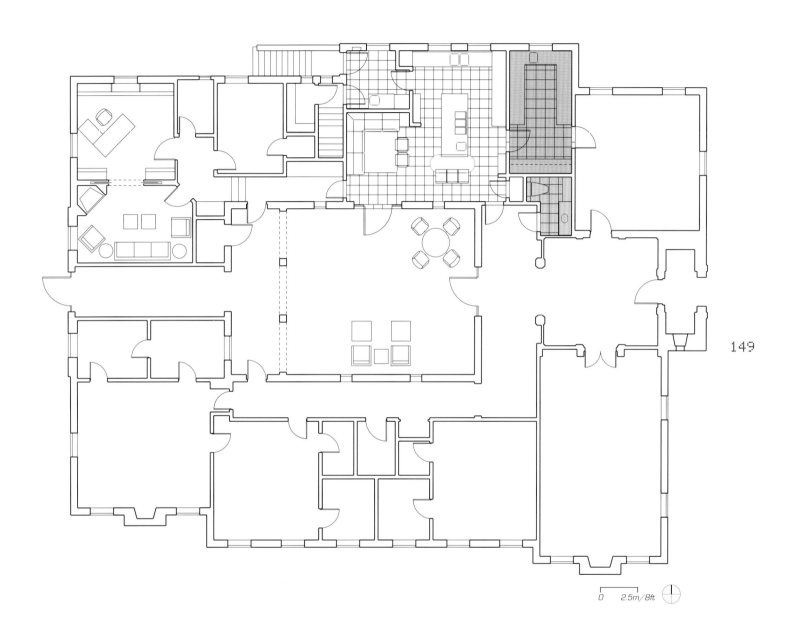

149

"Tall slender mirror and sconces accent floating glass basin" RONALD FRINK ARCHITECTS

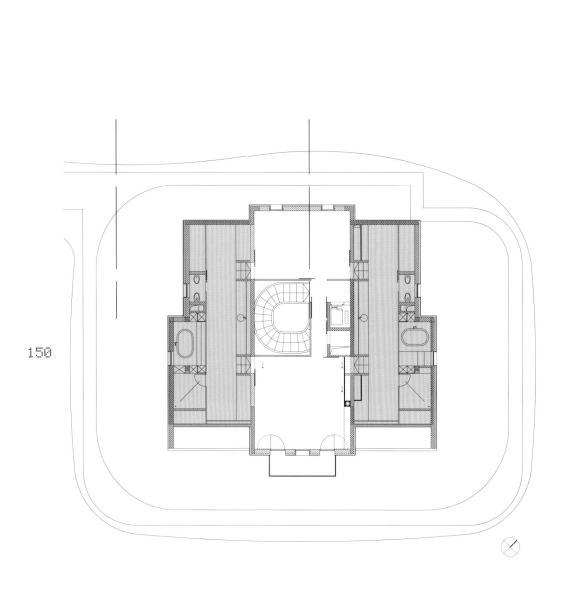

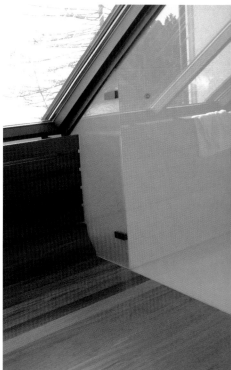

"Bath, shower, toilet, and washbasin are separate boxes on the left and right of the corridor…like on a train"
OFIS ARHITEKTI

"Glass mosaic tiles add richness to small spaces" STANIC HARDING

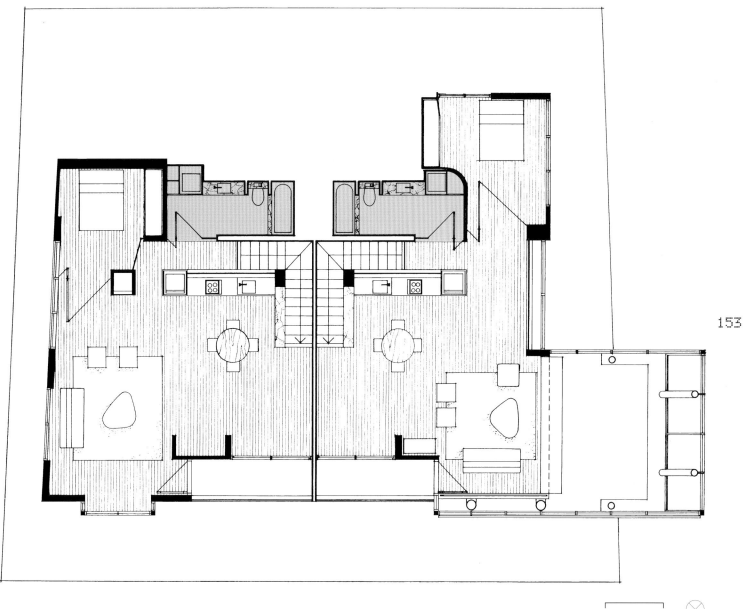

153

0   2m/6ft

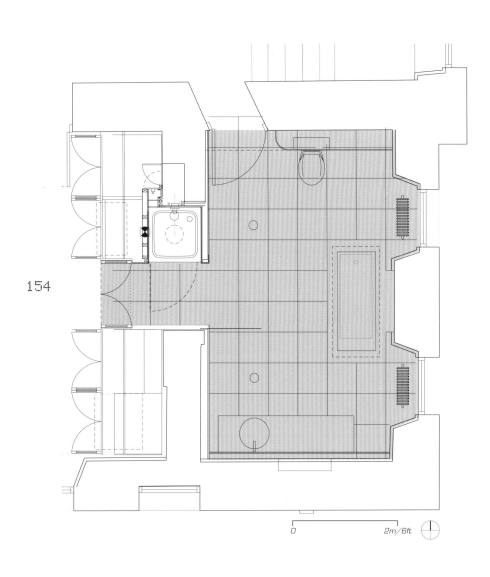

0   2m/6ft

"The bespoke recessed storage creates an uncluttered sanctuary" LEE BOYD

"Cool glass, warm stone, and rich wood impart an urban spa atmosphere" SHUBIN + DONALDSON ARCHITECTS

"The vanity hangs from the wall" MARK ENGLISH ARCHITECTS

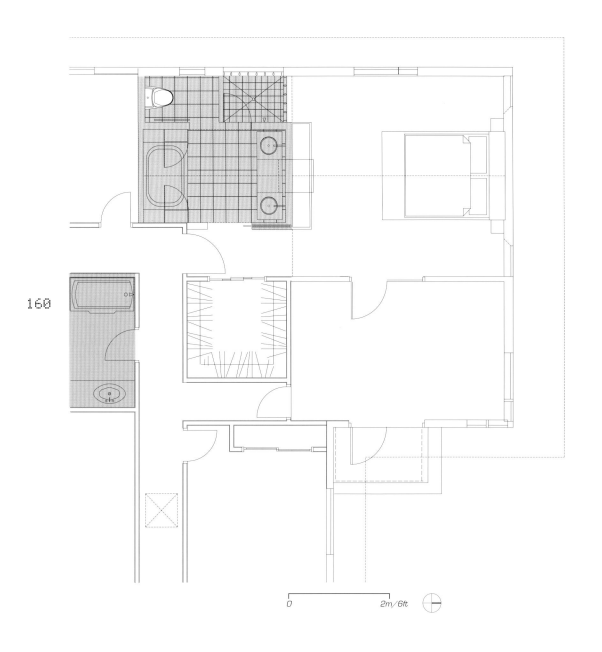

160

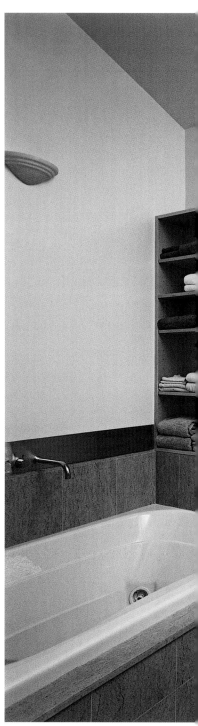

0   2m/6ft

"View of corridor through shower" AARDVARCHITECTURE

"Colored glass walls make internal spaces feel light" STANIC HARDING

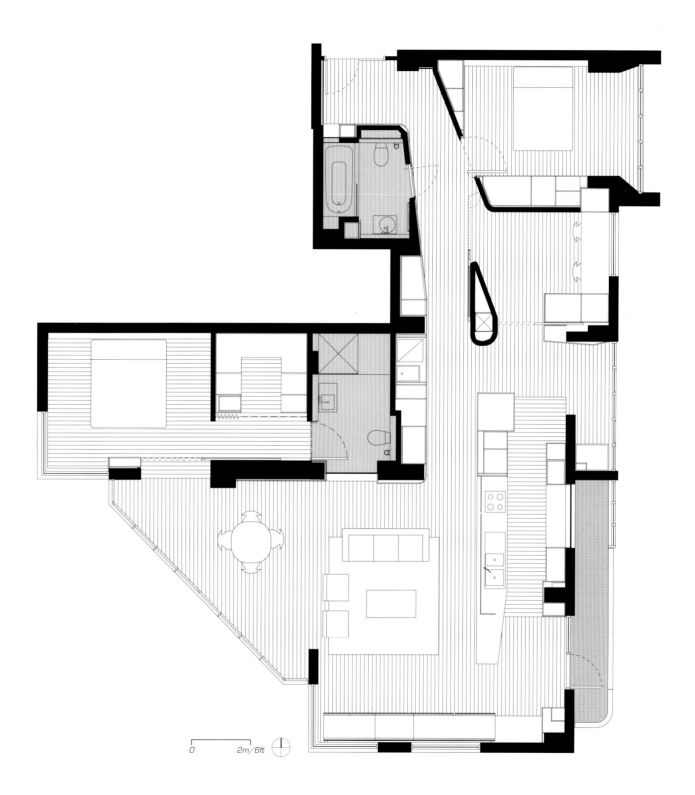

0   2m/6ft

"Combination of natural materials and mirrors makes an interesting palette" DAVID HICKS PTY LTD

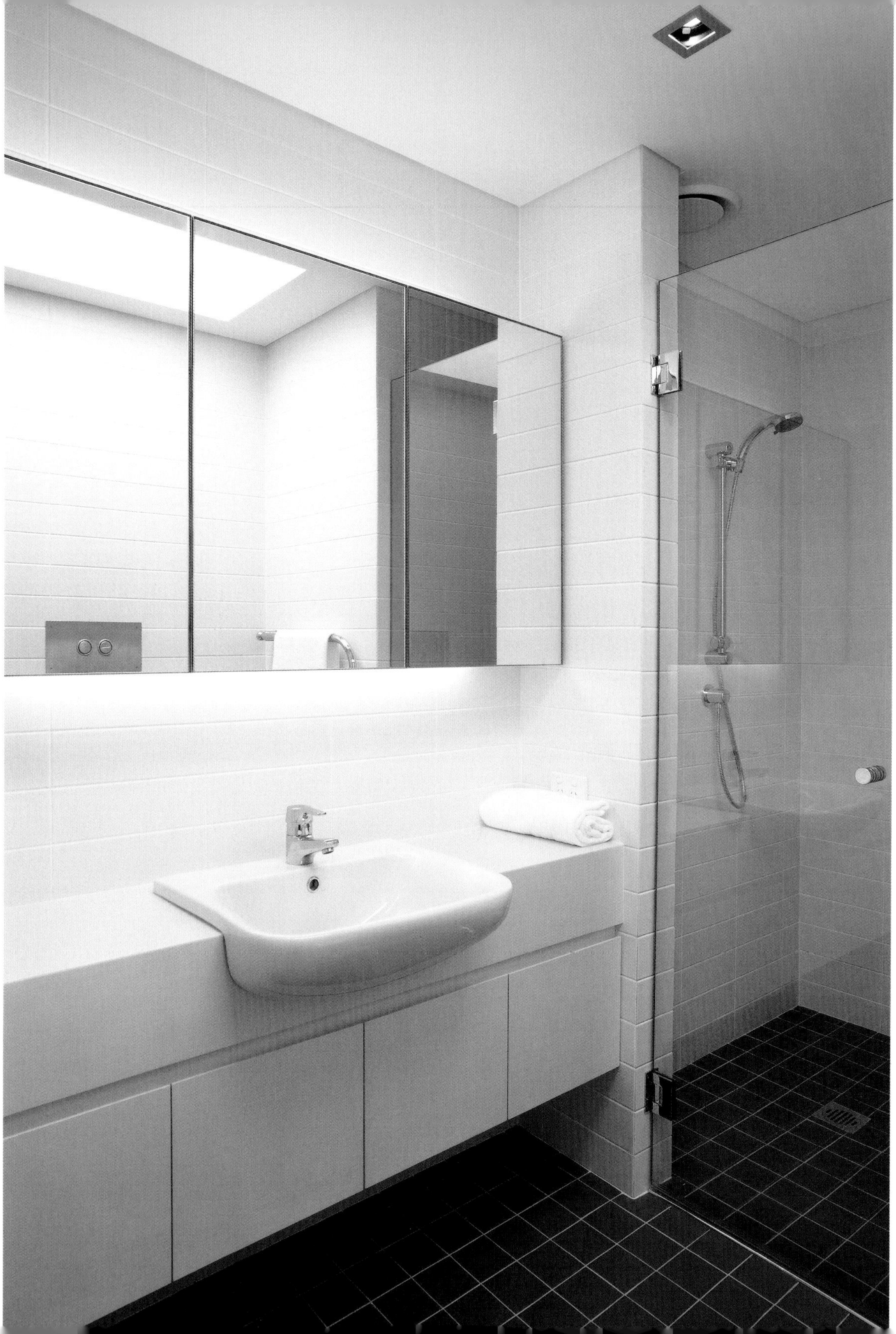

169

0   8m/26ft

"Skylight liberates walls and allows for full-height tiling" CULLEN FENG

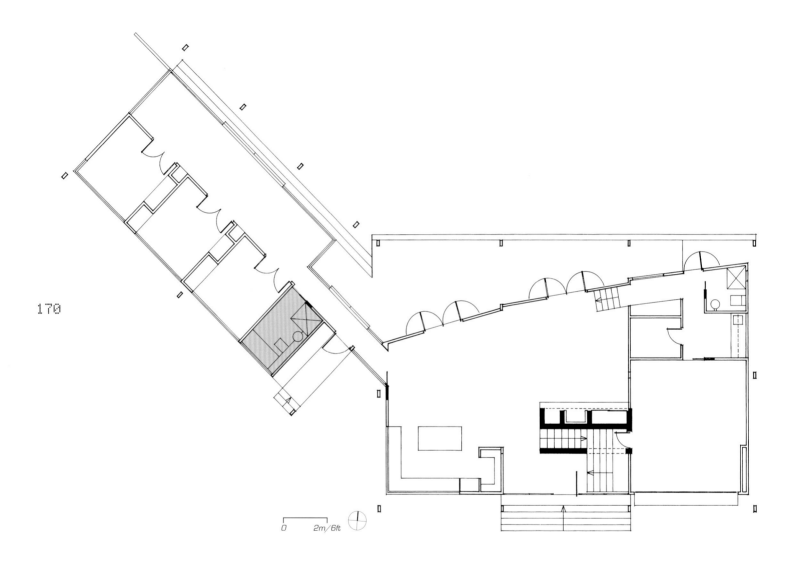

0   2m/6ft

"The fully-integrated sink captures all spills" CONNOR + SOLOMON

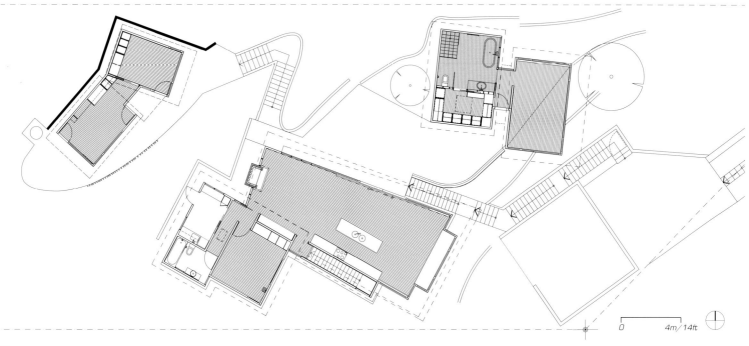

172

"Light fills the spacious bathroom from all sides" DAWSON BROWN ARCHITECTURE

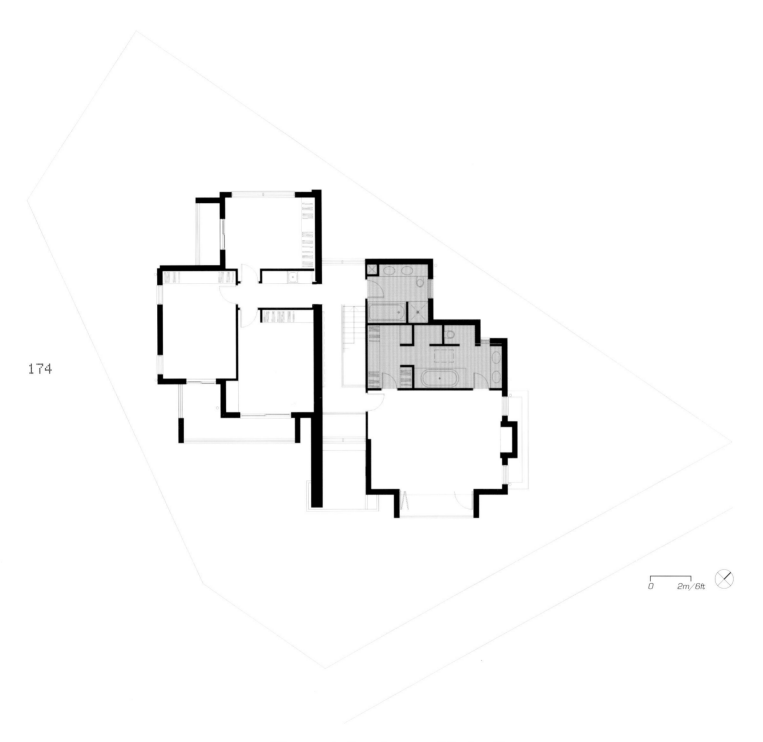

0   2m/6ft

"Shower and toilet enclosures are fully glazed" CORBEN

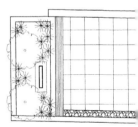

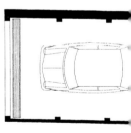

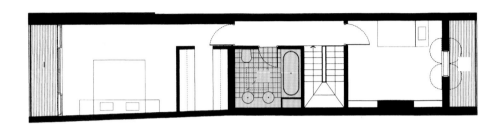

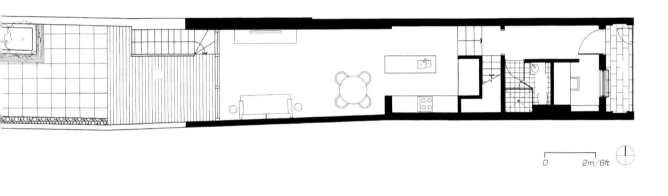

177

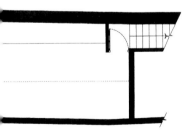

0   2m/6ft

"Floating vanity increases perceived space" CULLEN FENG

"The continuation of master bedroom circulation and cabinetry organizes the shower room" RESOLUTION:4 ARCHITECTURE

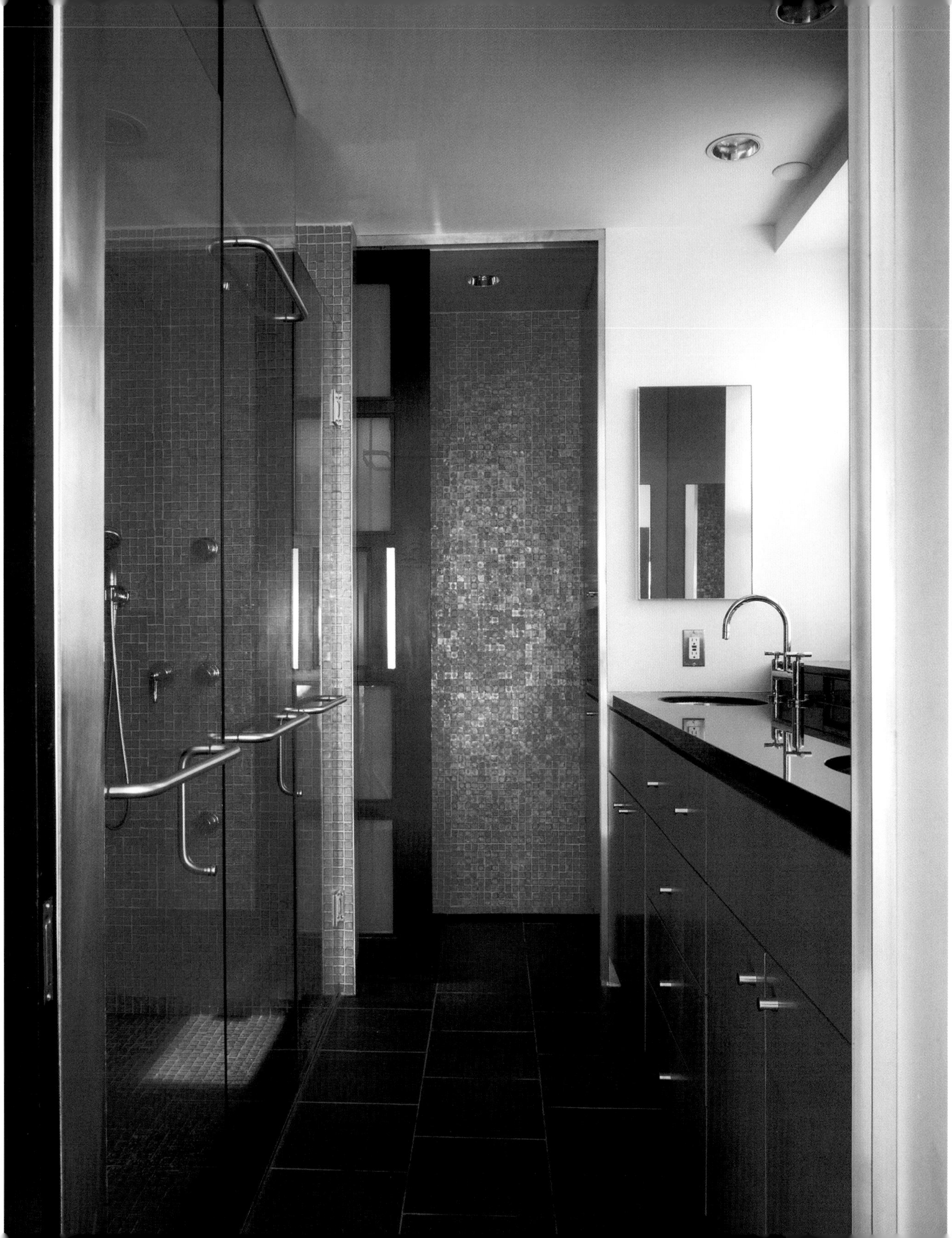

"Timber elements complement general bathroom finishes" STANIC HARDING

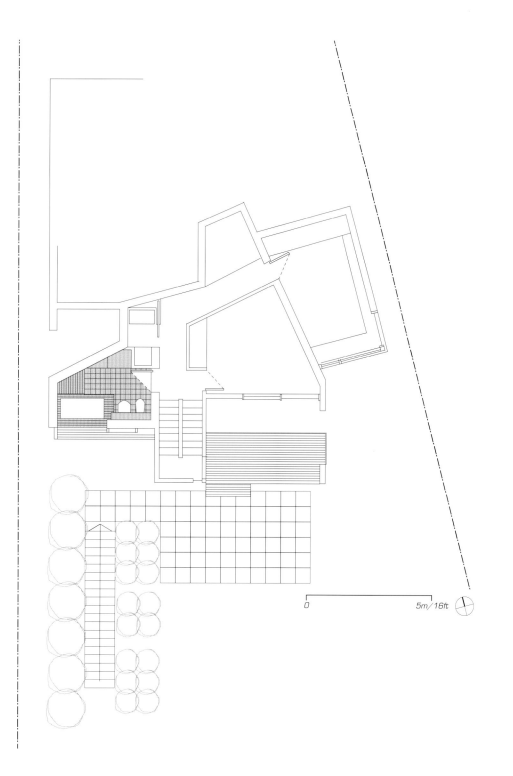

181

0   5m/16ft

182

"Light wood and textured marble ensure modern, yet warm feeling" MCINTOSH PORIS

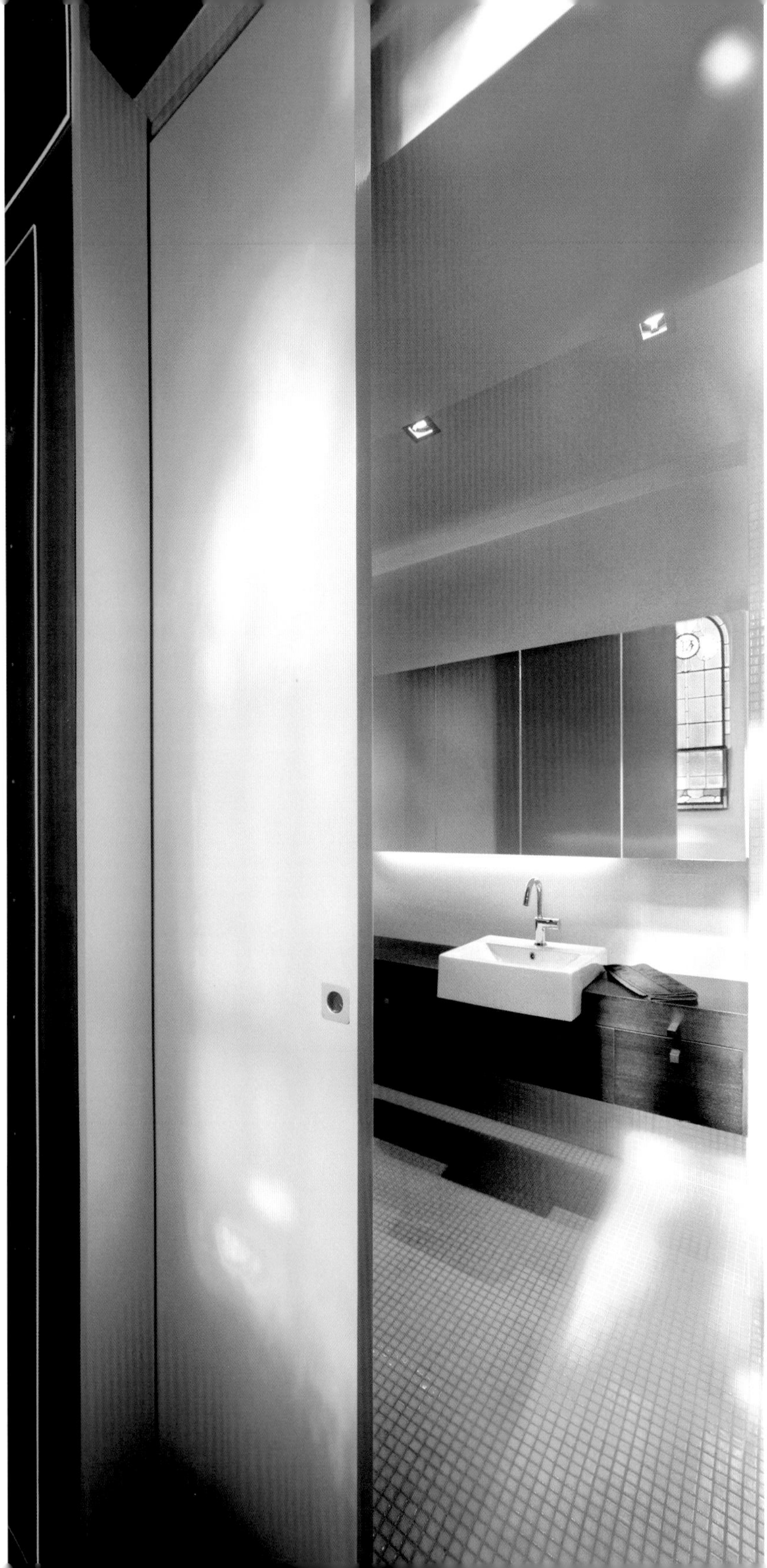

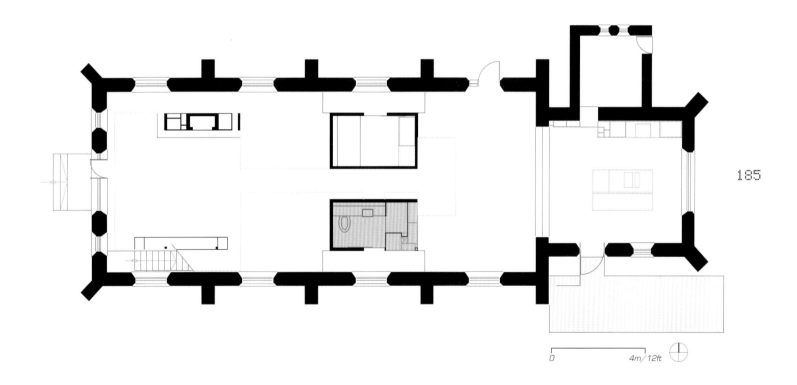

185

"Mirrors reflect original stained-glass window and enlarge the space" MULTIPLICITY

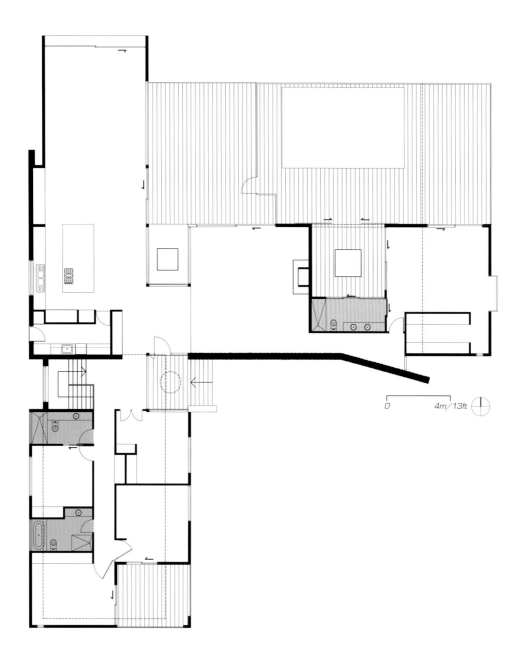

186

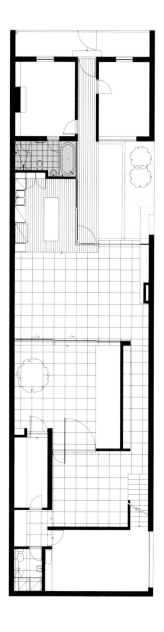

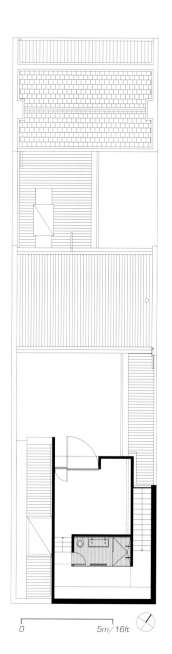

0   5m/16ft

"There is a strong physical or visual link with the outside" COY & YIONTIS

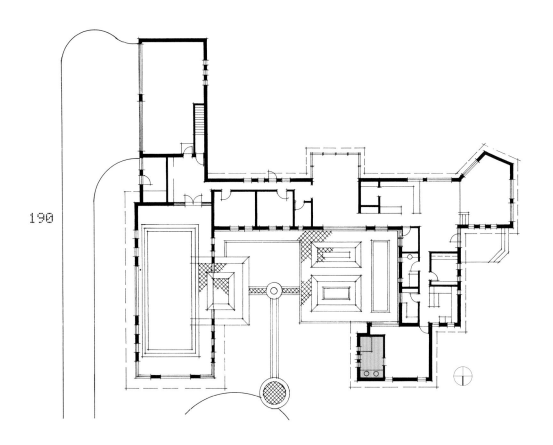

190

"Full-length stainless steel bench runs into the shower" SECCULL ARCHITECTS

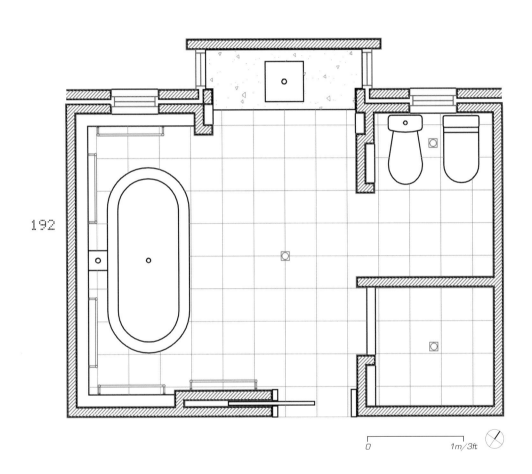

0   1m/3ft

"Subtle detailing, clean lines, and elegant bath create a sense of calm" CRAIG STEERE ARCHITECTS

"Shower is partly outside the building, giving a sensation of showering in the trees" STUTCHBURY PAPE

"Lit cubbyholes accommodate towels or other objects" SHUBIN + DONALDSON ARCHITECTS

"Central bathhouse allows views of the surrounding native plants" ELIZABETH & GABRIEL POOLE DESIGN COMPANY

"Sliding perforated screens provide a level of appropriate privacy" COL BANDY ARCHITECTS

"Creative use of one material: birch veneer plywood" ARCHIMANIA

"Stone and wood interact to create a sensuous tactility" CHA & INNERHOFER ARCHITECTURE + DESIGN

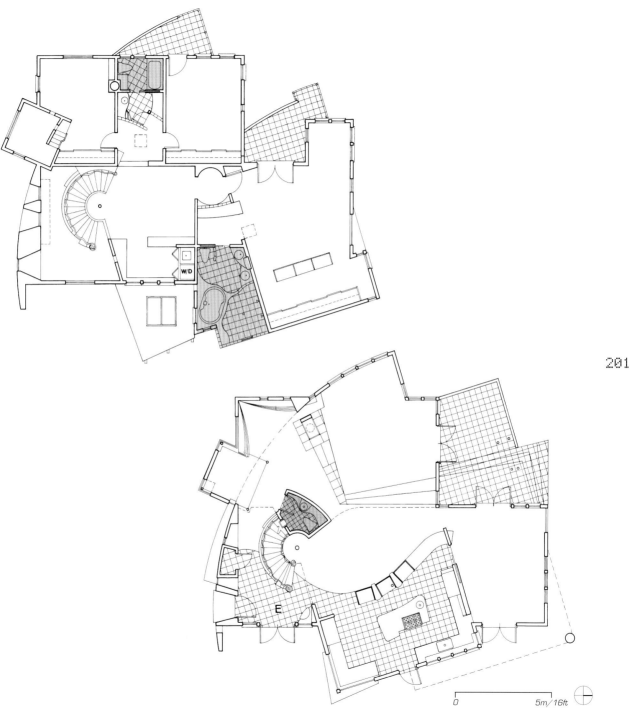

W/D

E

0   5m/16ft

"Sensual curving forms glisten with light and iridescent colors" HOUSE + HOUSE

"Fire-etched glass windows and doors allow light in, while maintaining privacy" SHUBIN + DONALDSON ARCHITECTS

"Backlit frosted-glass wall creates a greater sense of depth in a small room" SUPERKÜL INC ARCHITECT

"Areas are separated into wet and dry zones" BRIAN MEYERSON ARCHITECTS

"Elements float in a glazed lightwell" DALE JONES-EVANS PTY LTD ARCHITECTURE

"A soft palette of wood and concrete warms the sleek modern design" HOUSE + HOUSE

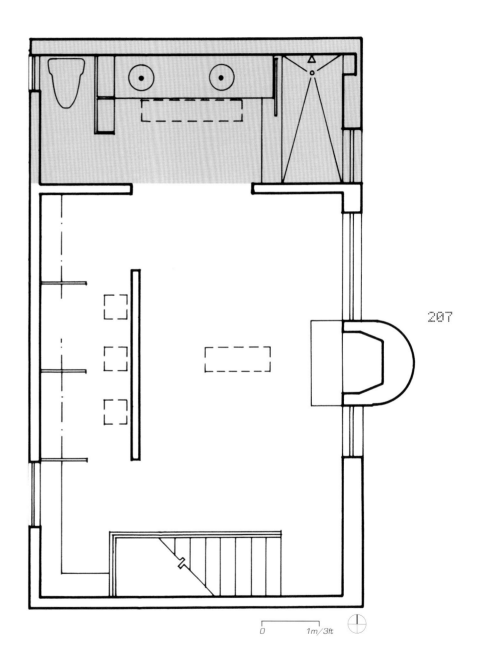

0   1m/3ft

"The bathroom's glass walls reflect light from the skylight" ENGELEN MOORE

"Light expansively links the bathroom to the outside" INTERLANDI MANTESSO ARCHITECTS

"*The bath has glass-box bookends that contain a toilet and shower respectively*" JACKSON CLEMENTS BURROWS ARCHITECTS

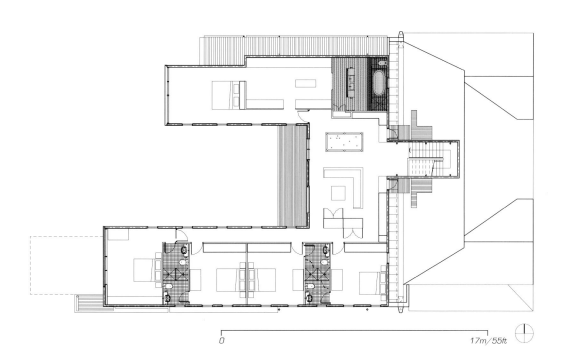

0   17m/55ft

212

"Materials flow from one space to another for seamless visual connections" OJMR

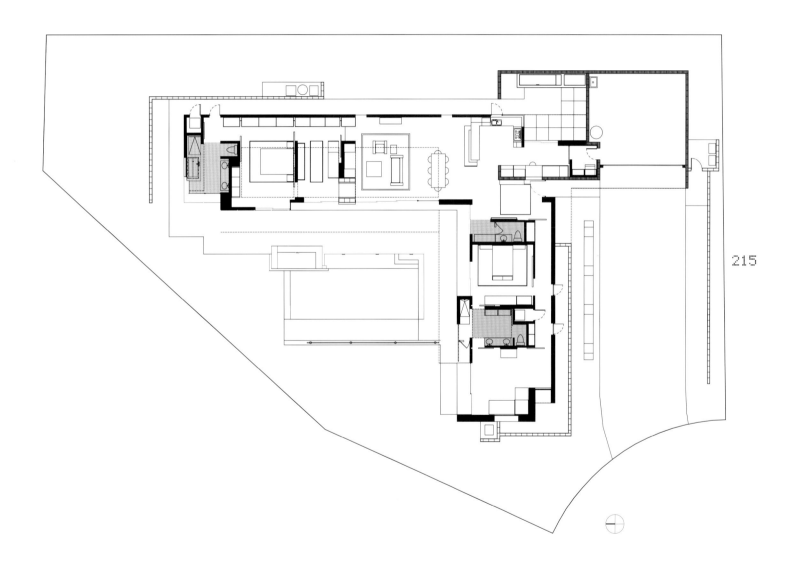

215

216

"The bather has a comfortable view of the outdoors" ELLIOTT + ASSOCIATES ARCHITECTS

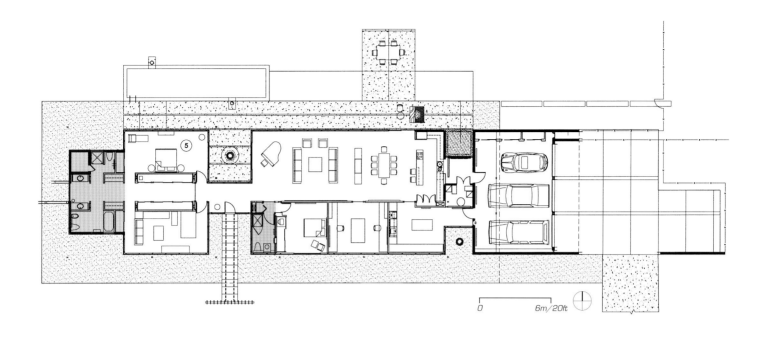

0   6m/20ft

218

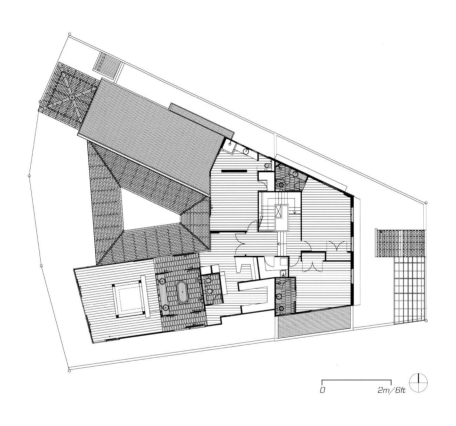

0   2m/6ft

"The materials are natural" BLIGH VOLLER NIELD PTY LTD

220

"Square basins complement the design" CCS ARCHITECTURE

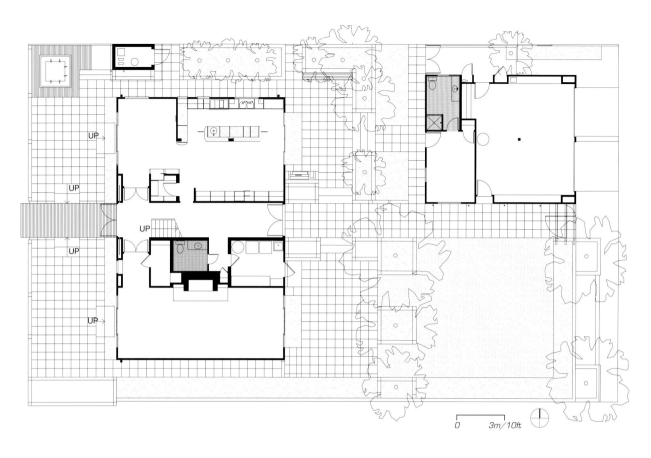

"A cubist composition in space and light" ALEXANDER GORLIN ARCHITECT

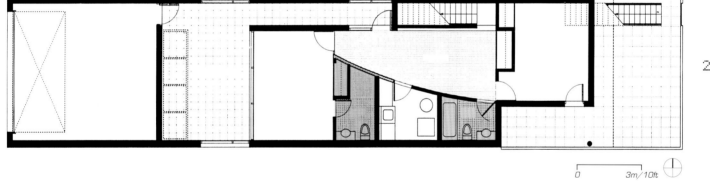

223

0   3m/10ft

"White marble slate creates a cool and calm setting" ALEXANDER GORLIN ARCHITECT

0   2m/6ft

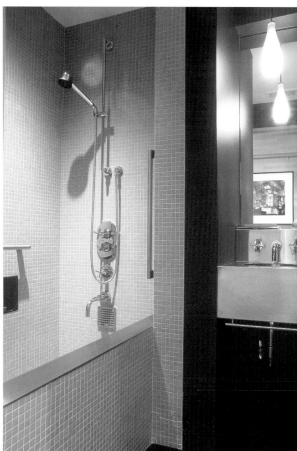

"Space is intimate" CCS ARCHITECTURE

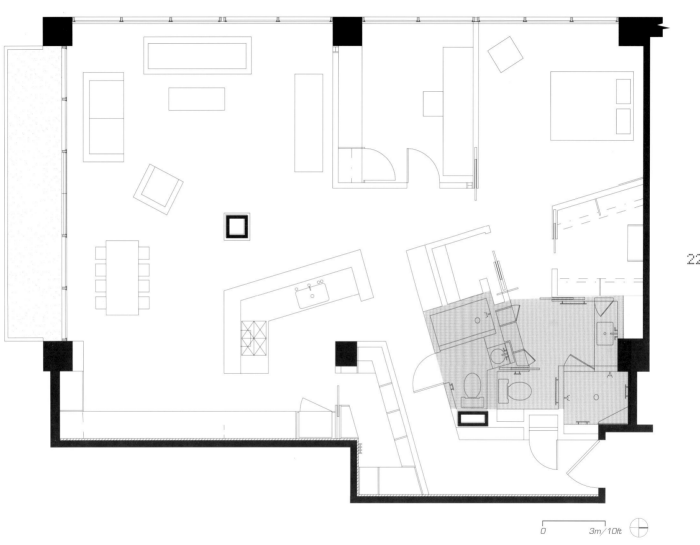

229

0   3m/10ft

"A broken tile mural links rough geometry to a long brick vault" HOUSE + HOUSE

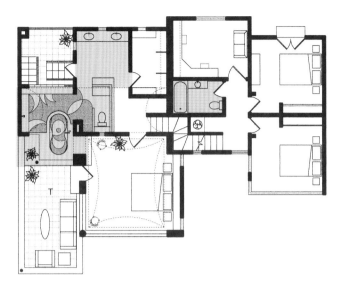

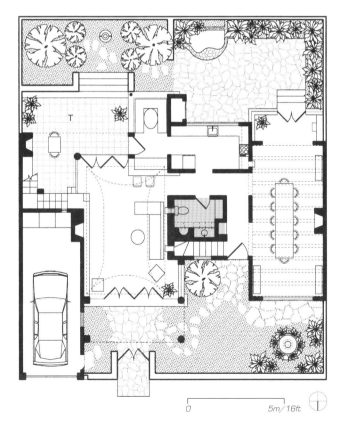

0   5m/16ft

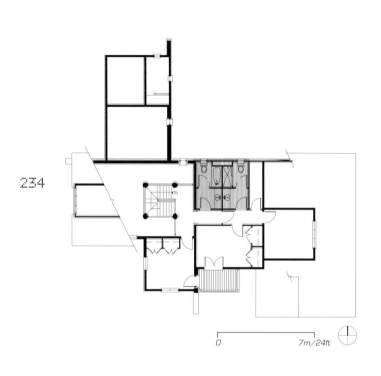

0   7m/24ft

"A simple bathroom with rustic features" DUBBE-MOULDER ARCHITECTS, PC

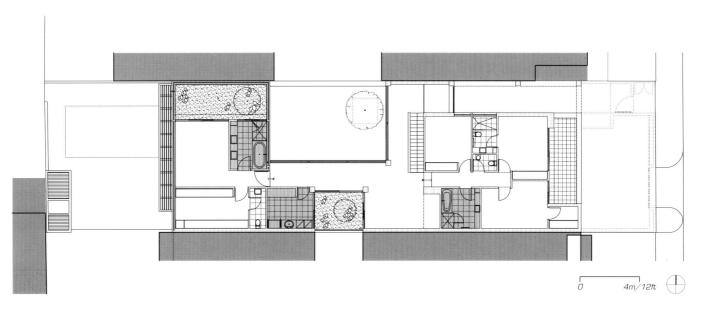

0   4m/12ft

"Framed view of partially hidden Magnolia" B.E. ARCHITECTURE

236

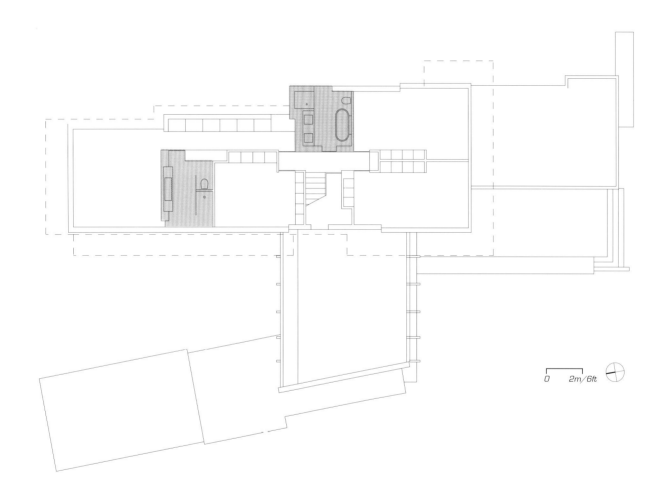

0   2m/6ft

"Space is intimate, with soft finishes and hidden utilities" MONCKTON FYFE

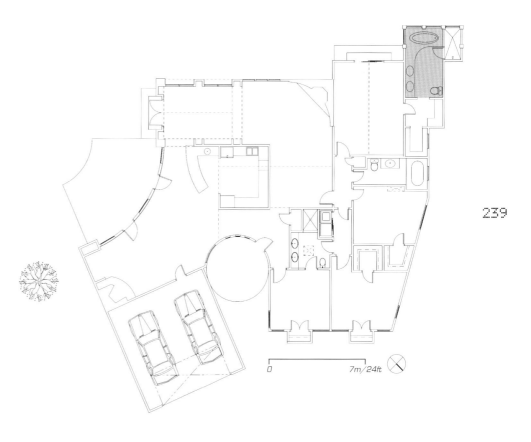

239

0   7m/24ft

"Designed around a unique curly-maple veneer" MARK ENGLISH ARCHITECTS

"Monochromatic use of materials and colors enhances the space" BBP ARCHITECTS

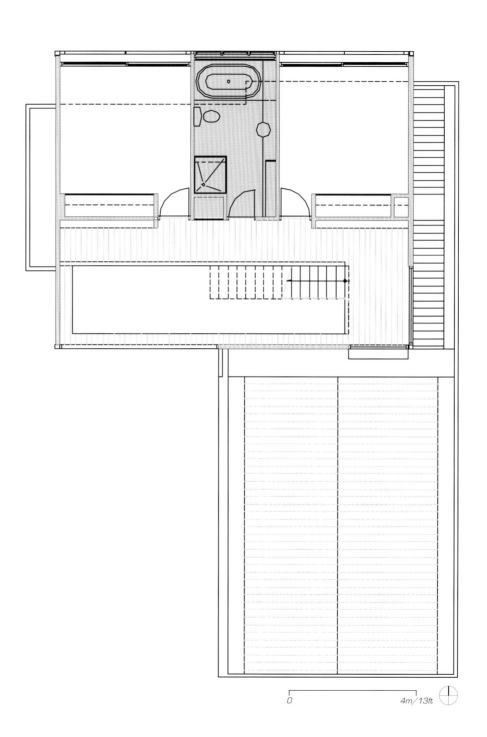

0   4m/13ft

"Reinvented veranda bathroom with mini-orb, timber, and recycled house components" JOHN MAINWARING & ASSOCIATES ARCHITECTS

"The use of marble makes for a sophisticated bathroom" OSKAR MIKAIL ARQUITETURA DE INTERIORS

Index of Architects

245

Index of Architects
continued

Index of Photographers

Index of Photographers
continued

252